HIGH POTENCY, HIGHER PROFIT

HIGH POTENCY, HIGHER PROFIT

Preeti Jain

Available on amazonkindle

Worldwide Published by

Pendown Press
PREMIUM BUSINESS PUBLISHER

PENDOWN PRESS LLP
An ISO 9001 & ISO 14001 Certified Co.,
Regd. Office: 3767A, Kanhaiya Nagar,
Tri Nagar, Delhi-110035
Ph.: 8130886000, 9650072927, 8595249536
E-mail: info@pendownpress.com
Branch Office: 1A/2A, 20, Hari Sadan, Ansari Road,
Daryaganj, New Delhi-110002
Ph.: 011-45794768
Website: PendownPress.com

Edition: 2025
Price: ₹ 399
ISBN: 978-93-6338-013-4

Layout and Cover Designed by Pendown Graphics Team
Printed and Bound in India by Thomson Press India Ltd.

Table of Contents

Invocation and Intention

'Sidhguruvar' Sidheshwar Brahmrishi Gurudev

"The One Who Saw Me Before I Could See Myself"

With my deepest reverence.

With complete surrender to the eternal light of my Gurudev — the one who gave to vision my darkness and words to my silence, and guided me on this sacred journey of service.

"गुरु कुम्हार शिष कुम्भ है, गढ़ि गढ़ि काढ़े खोट।
अंदर हाथ सहारे दे, बाहर मारे चोट॥" – Kabir

Translation:

The Guru is the potter, the disciple a clay pot.

With one hand within, He supports and shapes;

With the other, He strikes from outside to remove flaws.

My Gurudev is not just my guide – He is the very hands that shaped me.

In every storm, He was the stillness.

In every confusion, He was the compass.

When I strayed, He struck – not to hurt, but to correct.

When I broke, He held – from within, silently, so I could rise again.

Whatever is good in me today is His prasad. Whatever I may become is already His vision.

I do not walk this path alone— I am the vessel, He the breath that gives it purpose.

And now, through every word I speak, every work I offer –

He lights a lamp within me.

His flame does not burn; it reveals.

**It dissolves darkness, doubt, and the self that clings –
So only the truth may remain.**

He is the sun behind every sunrise in my life.

And I, just a flicker, carrying His light forward.

This book is not just about oils. It is about service — about purity, truth, and the potential for healing that lies dormant in the very seeds of nature.

In a world inundated with noise, we return to the prayer:

"सर्वे भवन्तु सुखिनः, सर्वे सन्तु निरामयाः।"

May all experience eternal bliss. May all thrive through a healed being, free from every illness.

And we are rooted in this unwavering truth:

"शरीरमाद्यं खलु धर्मसाधनम्।"

The body is the first instrument through which we fulfill our dharma.

From this place of reverence, we do not make products.

We offer intentions in the form of oils.

We press not for profit, but for purity. We heal, we honour, we serve.

Every drop that we bottle carries this vibration — a sacred reminder that health is not a transaction, it is transformation. Not a commodity, but a calling. This book, and the work we do at Vintage Aroma, is not just a business endeavor; it is a divine act of sacred alignment. A movement toward conscious commerce. A return to wholeness where nature, purpose, and prosperity coexist

This is my invocation.

This is our intention.

This is where it begins.

Gratitude to My Mentor

> To the one who shaped my vision into reality
> – Akshar Yadav Sir

There are teachers who impart knowledge, and then there are mentors who rewire your being.

Akshar Sir is the latter.

In a world that often equates progress with speed and noise, he taught me the stillness of strategic clarity. He refined the way I think, speak, write, and show up. Where others offer advice, he offers structure. Where others gave opinions, he gave a lens. His mentorship was not an event, but a realignment — the inner architecture that turned my passion into purpose.

It is because of his guidance that I could organize my vision into a tangible offering. Because of him, I could begin to serve not just as a manufacturer of oils, but as an educator, a healer, and a bridge between nature's truth and the world's need.

This chapter is a bow to him — to the power of discipline, structure, and conscious marketing. His presence echoes in every framework, every articulation, every clarity that follows in this book.

Thank you, Sir.

Chapter 1

The Myth

Fats Are Unhealthy

We've been told a lie!

A deeply embedded one.

- That fats are bad.
- That they make us fat, sick, and sluggish.
- That cutting them out is the path to health.

For decades, this myth has ruled mainstream diets, marketing campaigns, and misguided health advice. And we, unknowingly, obeyed.

But here is the truth

Not all fats are created equal.

And not all of them are harmful.

In fact, the right fats, when consumed consciously, in the right form and from the right source, are among the most vital nutrients your body needs to function, heal, and thrive.

Why, then, did this myth gain such power and popularity?

Because the world industrialized food. It commodified nourishment. It replaced purity with processing, and in that shift, good fats were lumped together with harmful trans fats and ultra-refined oils.

The consequence?

Generations of fatigue, brain fog, hormonal imbalance, low immunity, and rising mental health concerns.

This chapter opens the curtain on **unlearning and relearning**. It breaks the trance that this myth has kept us in.

And it invites you to ask:

Could the very thing we were taught to avoid... be the missing link to performance, vitality, and clarity?

It's time to separate the myth from real substance.

It's time to wake up.

To unlearn the noise. And remember what the body always knew—before the world told it to forget.

Chapter 2

The Body is Built on Fat

Fats are not enemies — they are the foundation of our existence.

Our brain is nearly 60% fat.

Every neuron, every cell membrane, and every hormone synthesis pathway is reliant on the presence of lipids. From the curve of your thoughts to the strength of your immune system, fat plays a silent but central role.

The real question isn't "Should I consume fat?" but rather: "Which fats, and in what form, fuel my best self?"

This chapter explores the biology of fat, from omega chains to cell regeneration, from inflammation control to cognitive performance.

Good fats stabilize mood, balance hormones, and help regenerate neurons. Bad fats, on the other hand, increase oxidative stress and create silent inflammation.

What unfolds in these pages is:

- How fats are structured and why it matters
- The role of essential fatty acids
- Fat-soluble vitamins and their absorption

- Why your brain, skin, gut, and hormones rely on fat for function

Let's rebuild your relationship with fat, not as an indulgence, but as core infrastructure.

Understanding Good Fats vs Bad Fats

Not all fats are the same. The confusion around fats often arises because they are lumped into one category, but **in reality, their source, structure, and processing determine whether they heal or harm.**

Good Fats

- Unrefined, cold-pressed oils (like flaxseed, chia, black cumin, hemp, coconut)
- Rich in essential fatty acids (Omega 3, 6, and 9)
- Support cell regeneration, hormone production, and cognitive function
- Carry anti-inflammatory and antioxidant properties

Bad Fats

- Refined, hydrogenated, or repeatedly heated oils
- Contain trans fats or oxidized lipids
- Lead to inflammation, hormone disruption, and oxidative stress

The single most important factor that determines whether a fat is good or bad is how it is processed.

Check whether the oils you use follow the ancient art of single cold pressing under controlled temperature, preserving the natural structure, aroma, and therapeutic compounds.

At Vintage Aroma, we follow this process strictly.

Key Markers of Good Fats

- **Naturally occurring aroma and taste** *(Signals purity and lack of deodorization)*
- **Rich color and less viscosity** *(Indicates minimal processing and intact micronutrients)*
- **Low acidity** *(Sign of freshness and proper seed handling)*
- **High antioxidant stability** *(Due to natural tocopherols, polyphenols, and phytosterols)*
- **Cold-pressed under controlled temperature** *(Preserves molecular structure and active compounds)*
- **Single-pressed, not re-extracted** *(Ensures maximum nutrient density from first press only)*
- **Free from chemical solvents and preservatives** *(Truly natural and unadulterated)*
- **Quick seed-to-bottle processing** *(Reduces oxidation, preserves vitality)*
- **Bottled in dark glass or non-reactive containers** *(Prevents light- and heat-induced degradation)*
- **Traceable origin and seed variety** *(Confidence in the oil's therapeutic potential and consistency)*

This information will help you in:

- Identifying true good fats on labels
- Understanding "*rotary press*" vs "Single Cold-pressed" vs "refined"
- Making conscious, informed choices in sourcing and consuming fats

A good fat doesn't just nourish your body — it respects your biology.

Chapter 3

Fats Fuel Performance

The New Energy Paradigm

What Powers a Peak Performer?

- ➢ Is it the coffee we drink at 9 AM?
- ➢ The energy bar we reach for at 4 PM?
- ➢ The sugar rush before a meeting?

Or could the real answer be more fundamental... more biological?

The truth is, our most sustainable energy source is:

❌ Not sugar.

❌ It's not caffeine.

✅ It's **fat.**

Why Fats Trump Caffeine and Sugar?

Unlike sugar, which offers a quick high followed by a sharp crash, fats, **especially medium-chain triglycerides and essential fatty acids, provide a slow-release, stable form of energy that powers the body and brain throughout the day.**

When your body is trained to burn fat efficiently (a process known as fat-adaptation, a form of metabolic adjustment), it switches from burning glucose to using fat for fuel.

This creates

- Better **mental clarity**
- Longer **attention span**
- Lower **fatigue**
- Enhanced **emotional resilience**

Energy Source	**Spike**	**Crash**	**Long Term Impact**
Caffeine	⚡	😴	Adrenalin Fatigue, Dependency
Refined Sugar	⚡⚡	😴😴	Insulin Resistance, Brain Fog
Good Fats	🌿	❌	Sustained Clarity, Hormonal Balance

- Caffeine is a whip.
- Sugar is a rush.
- **Fat is a sustained-release flow**.

Cold-Pressed Oils and Brain Power

The brain is nearly 60% fat.

If your brain is the CEO of your body, then fat is its power supply.

And when the source of that fat is potent, clean, and conscious, performance becomes inevitable.

Most people reach for caffeine to combat fatigue.

Some rely on sugar to power through slumps.

But the truly sustainable fuel for mental clarity, emotional balance, and physical stamina lies in the right kind of fat.

When you feed it high-quality fats like Omega-3 rich Chia seed oil, Thymoquinone-rich Black Cumin Seed Oil, or MCTs from Coconut Oil:

- You support neuroplasticity (your brain's ability to learn and adapt)
- You balance neurotransmitters like serotonin and dopamine
- You reduce cortisol levels, keeping stress in check

The Science of Fueling the Brain

Your brain is nearly 60% fat, and the fatty acids in your diet directly influence:

- Cognition
- Focus
- Memory
- Mood

Essential fatty acids such as DHA (an omega-3) are crucial for neuron structure and communication.

Deficiency leads to brain fog, anxiety, and low emotional resilience.

Good Fats

- Stabilize glucose (no sugar crashes)
- Reduce inflammation (especially in the brain)
- Support neurotransmitter production

Fats don't give you a spike. They give you stamina.

Fats & Productivity: How They Work

When your neurons are coated with healthy fat (myelin), signals move faster.

You think faster. Remember more. React sharper.

Good Fats Also

- Support the **gut-brain axis**
- Enhance **hormonal balance** (especially cortisol and serotonin)
- Improve **sleep quality** and **stress recovery**

When your brain is calm, your output amplifies.

Cognitive Work Needs Cognitive Fuel

In a 2024 workplace nutrition study, **teams using cold-pressed oils experienced**:

- **20% lower post-lunch fatigue**
- **17% fewer sick days**
- **25% increase in self-reported focus**

What Changed?

- Not the deadlines.
- Not the team structure.
- Just the **quality of fat** in daily meals.

Why This Matters for Performance

Your mitochondria — the energy factories inside every cell — rely heavily on **healthy fats** to function efficiently. When fed with poor-quality, oxidized oils, they slow down. But when powered by clean, cold-pressed fats, they:

- Burn fuel more efficiently
- Repair faster
- Delay biological aging

This is why elite athletes, creative professionals, and forward-thinking companies are now focusing on **fat-driven performance** strategies.

Everyday Performance, Elevated

The oils we consume can make the difference between:

- **Midday crashes** vs **high mental stamina**
- **Bloating** vs **lightness**
- **Irritability** vs **groundedness**
- **Brain fog** vs **sharp focus**
- **Frequent sick days** vs **resilient immunity**
- **Dry, dull skin** vs **hydrated glow**
- **Hormonal fluctuations** vs **emotional balance**
- **Sluggish mornings** vs **sustained energy**

- **Cravings and overeating** vs **satiety and nourishment**
- **Digestive heaviness** vs **gut comfort and regularity**

At Vintage Aroma, we've observed this shift in hundreds of clients:

- Better morning energy
- Deeper focus at work
- Reduced PMS and hormonal disturbances
- Fewer sick days

All from switching to single-pressed oils that retain their therapeutic spectrum.

Good fats don't just feed your cells.

They elevate your state.

Fats as the Conscious Alternative to Stimulants

Let's be honest — caffeine, sugar, and quick carbs are overstimulating shortcuts.

Fats, however, offer foundational resilience.

- They don't just push you forward — they **help you rise without crashing.**
- They anchor your nervous system.
- They fuel your *presence.*

With this information, we're not just redefining energy. We're redesigning **how we live, work, and perform.**

The question is no longer "Do fats give you energy?" It's: **"Can you afford to perform without them?"**

Chapter 4

Why I Do What I Do – My Calling

The Journey That Pressed Me Into Purpose

Now that we have been discussing and debunking myths about fats, their benefits, how to choose them, and how they should be processed, etc., I'm sure you're wondering...

Who am I to know so much about oils?

Well, I'm not a nutritionist who read it in a textbook. I'm not a marketer spinning a health claim.

I'm someone who lives this knowledge every single day.

From standing on sunny, dusty farms selecting seeds with farmers...

To personally overseeing the pressing of every batch of oil in our factory...

To sitting across the table from scientists, chefs, formulators, and health pioneers...

I've spent the last 18 years decoding the journey from seed to cell—how functional oils, when pressed right and chosen wisely, can truly transform the body, the brain, and even a business.

My name is Preeti Jain.

And this—fats, oils, truth, and transformation—is my life's work.

In 2007, I didn't set out to become a manufacturer. I set out to understand the truth.

It began with one small fabricated machine, borrowed space, and a heart full of questions.

I stood at the edge of fields, listening to farmers, watching seeds, and wondering what we had forgotten.

What I discovered changed everything.

We had forgotten the **value of the seed**, not just as a commodity, but as a **living library** of nature's intelligence.

We had forgotten **that food could heal** — if only we didn't kill it in the name of shelf life.

We had forgotten that oils were **supposed to be alive.**

Cold-pressed oil wasn't a trend for me.
It was my calling.

The German Buyer Who Changed My Life

One moment shaped my direction. A German client once told me:

"Only apply on the skin what you can safely eat."

It echoed deeply. Because in Ayurveda, it was already known. And now science was catching up.

This single idea became my litmus test.

- Would I feed this oil to a child?
- Would I apply it to my own skin?

If the answer wasn't a full-bodied yes, we wouldn't bottle it.

I faced crop failures, financial strain, and skepticism from the market.

But with every drop pressed, I pressed on.

In 2012, we rented a proper factory.

By 2017, we had a fully certified unit — ISO, FSSAI, NOP Organic.

Today, we export oil across the world.

But what never changed was the purpose.

A Commitment to Integrity & Purity

"When I began formulating my therapeutic skincare line, **I wasn't just looking for oils—I was searching for the purest, most vibrant good fats that could carry healing actives deep into the skin and amplify their effect.** I insisted, and **Vintage Aroma listened.**

On my request, they began pressing exquisite oils like Moringa, Jojoba, and Radish Seed, and **what they delivered went far beyond expectation. These are not just raw materials; they are living, intelligent carriers of therapeutic energy.**

What truly sets Vintage Aroma apart is their unwavering commitment to integrity—they have even crafted their own machinery to ensure that the oil's quality is never compromised at any level. From seed selection to bottling, they have mastered every stage of the journey, delivering purity, consistency, and seamless service.

Their craftsmanship, patience, and devotion to quality have made them an irreplaceable part of Akari's healing philosophy. **My formulations simply wouldn't carry the same depth without their oils."**

Ingrid Harrant
Founder, Akari – Nature's Secret, Austria

This Is Not Just Business. It's *Seva* (Service).

Service to Nature. Service to Health. Service to Truth.

When I press oils today, I don't just see seeds. I see **farmers' hands, earth's memory,** and **the imprint of divine design**.

This isn't about black cumin or chia or jojoba alone. It's about **restoring a broken relationship between humanity and food**.

I write this book to share my journey, not because I am important, but because the mission is.

I want you all–as the formulators, the wellness brands, the conscious buyers–to feel what I feel when I open a new batch:

That we are not merely in the business of selling oils. We are in the business of awakening.

Chapter 5

Plant-Based Fats
Nature's Design for Healing

In the search for optimal health, nature has always held the answer.

Fats from the animal kingdom have long dominated the dietary conversation — butter, ghee, tallow, fish oil — but the world is shifting. And not just for environmental or ethical reasons. The shift is grounded in science, performance, sustainability, and resonance with the human body.

Plant-based fats are not just alternatives. They are the original blueprints.

Why Plant-Based Fats?

- **Bioavailable**: Easily absorbed and processed by the body, without putting undue pressure on the liver or digestive system.
- **Functional**: Carry natural phytonutrients, antioxidants, and essential fatty acids.
- **Adaptogenic**: Often balance rather than overstimulate the body.
- **Versatile**: Can be consumed, applied, or formulated into products for targeted support.

- **Sustainable**: Lower carbon footprint, eco-conscious cultivation, and non-exploitative sourcing.

Understanding the Plant-Based Powerhouses

These oils do more than just nourish — they heal:

- **Black Cumin Seed Oil**: A treasure of thymoquinone, with anti-inflammatory, antioxidant, and immune-modulating properties.
- **Chia Seed Oil**: Packed with Omega-3 ALA, promoting heart and brain health.
- **Hemp Seed Oil**: Balances Omega 3 and 6 in an ideal ratio for cellular health and hormonal support.
- **Flaxseed Oil**: Supports cardiovascular function and hormonal balance.
- **Moringa Oil**: Rejuvenates skin and is rich in oleic acid and natural antiseptics.
- **Coconut Oil**: Offers quick metabolic energy via MCTs and supports gut flora.
- **Sweet Almond Oil**: Rich in Vitamin E and perfect for skin regeneration.

The Philosophy Behind Plant-Based Healing

It's Not Just What You Eat. It's What You Absorb.

In the world of wellness, we often obsess over *what* we eat—superfoods, supplements, organic produce. But the real secret to healing lies in something far simpler, yet far more powerful:

Absorption.

Plant-based oils aren't just nutrients.

They're *nutrient activators.*

They create what's known as **cofactor synergy**—a biological partnership that enables your body to absorb fat-soluble vitamins like **A, D, E, and K.**

Without these good fats:

- **That premium multivitamin?** It may pass right through you.
- **Your leafy greens?** Might not deliver their full antioxidant power.
- **That turmeric shot?** It could lose its anti-inflammatory edge.

This is the missing link in most health journeys. Healing isn't about how much you consume. It's about how much your body can *actually* use.

That's the true gift of cold-pressed plant oils.

Not just nourishment. But *activation.*

These oils do not *force* outcomes.

They *invite* balance.

In Ayurveda, fat is known as sneha, which also means love.

It's no coincidence. Fat is the carrier of nourishment, warmth, and deep tissue healing. When this carrier is derived from plants, from life that has photosynthesized the sun, it carries the intelligence of nature.

As modern science validates what ancient cultures always knew, we are witnessing a return to the real source of wellness — the **functional, sacred, and intentional use of plant fats**.

A Quiet Revolution

What was once called a "home remedy" is now at the forefront of nutraceutical research.

Cold-pressed seed oils, when extracted consciously, are not just food; they are functional medicine.

And plant fats are not trends. They are the foundation of a new health economy. **One that rewards conscious performance over chemical quick-fixes.**

In the chapters ahead, we'll see how these fats, especially Black Cumin Seed Oil, are transforming formulations, outcomes, and profit margins for forward-thinking brands.

But first, let us understand the role of fats as **functional ingredients** in the next chapter.

Purity That a Doctor Recommends Wholeheartedly

A bad cooking oil is worse than smoking—that's something I see all too often in clinical practice.

Fats are fundamental to our health, and the oils we use every day can either support or silently harm our well-being.

I've seen real improvements in patients' lipid profiles and inflammation markers when they switch to cold-pressed oils that retain their natural structure."

"Personally, I use a combination of Vintage Aroma's oils. Their cold-pressed mustard oil is my go-to for daily cooking—it offers essential unoxidized omega-6 while maintaining a good omega-3:6 balance, **which helps with energy, metabolism, and heart health. I also use their Black Cumin Seed Oil and Hemp Seed Oil regularly for their therapeutic benefits."**

"I believe rotating clean, high-quality oils brings a better balance to the body. Vintage Aroma's oils make that easy, with the kind of purity and consistency I'm comfortable recommending to health-conscious individuals, even those with cardiac concerns."

- Dr. Ravinder Singh Rao

Vice Chairman, RHL Jaipur

Chairman, RHL Heart Centre

Chapter 6

Functional Fats

More Than Nutrition, They Are Intervention

In the world of wellness, a quiet revolution is underway. And at its heart lie **functional fats** — oils that go beyond basic nutrition and perform specific roles in healing, regeneration, and optimization of body systems.

What Are Functional Fats?

These are plant-based oils that:

- Exhibit targeted therapeutic properties
- Aid in the prevention and management of chronic conditions
- Interact intelligently with your biology
- Support both structural health (cells, membranes) and dynamic function (hormones, cognition, immunity)

From Ingredient to Intervention

Think of the difference between salt and turmeric.

Salt enhances flavor.

Turmeric heals.

Functional fats are the turmeric of the oil world. They **intervene**, **restore**, and **amplify performance** at a cellular level.

Examples include:

- **Black Cumin Seed Oil** (Nigella Sativa): Anti-inflammatory, immune-modulating, brain-protective
- **Chia Seed Oil**: Rich in Omega-3 ALA for heart, mood, and gut health
- **Hemp Seed Oil**: Ideal Omega 3:6 ratio, hormonal balance, skin nourishment
- **Coconut Oil**: MCTs for metabolic energy and gut healing
- **Flaxseed Oil**: Hormonal support and cardiovascular health
- **Moringa Oil**: Antioxidant-rich and skin-rejuvenating
- and numerous other oils.

What Makes an Oil Functional?

It begins with the **seed**, and is completed by the **process**.

A functional oil doesn't happen by accident. It requires precision, purity, and purpose at every step.

It starts with the seed:

- **Only whole, unbroken seeds** are used
- **Zero foreign particles or impurities**
- **Sourced ethically and stored with care**
- **Grown for potency, not just yield**

Because if the seed is compromised, the oil is compromised.

Then comes the process:

- **Single cold pressing** (no re-extraction, no heat damage)
- **Temperature-controlled extraction** to preserve enzymatic and antioxidant activity
- **No solvents, no hexane, no preservatives**
- **Clean, traceable sourcing and storage**
- **Fast seed-to-bottle transition** to avoid oxidative loss

When oil is made this way, it is **alive**.

It carries **bioactive intelligence**, **structural integrity**, and **functional healing power**– not just for the body, but for the mind and skin too.

Functional Fats Support:

- Brain plasticity and neural repair
- Hormonal signaling and emotional balance
- Gut flora integrity
- Skin barrier protection
- Cell membrane flexibility
- Immune homeostasis

In short, they help the body respond better to life.

From Kitchen to Clinic

Functional fats blur the line between **nutrition and nutraceuticals**.

They are now being explored in:

- Brain health supplements
- Gut repair blends
- Hormonal balance therapies
- Natural anti-inflammatory solutions
- Oncology adjunct protocols
- Skin regeneration serums

And their applications are only growing.

A New Business Paradigm

This chapter isn't just for the health-conscious consumer.

It's a wake-up call for the entire wellness economy.

It speaks to:

- **Formulators** seeking to elevate the efficacy of their products
- **Retailers** who serve discerning, conscious buyers

- **Wellness clinics** uniting traditional healing with modern protocols
- **Exporters** ready to lead in the high-value, high-impact oil category

Because **functional fats are not mere commodities.**

They are **catalysts** for human vitality and for business transformation.

When you choose high-integrity oils, you're not just adding an ingredient.

You're investing in **better outcomes** and **profitable growth.**

High Integrity: Higher Benefits

"At APEX, we serve diverse importers with Black Seed Oil and soft gels—both gelatin and vegan. **And for all of it, we trust only one source: Vintage Aroma. Their quality is not just consistent; it is sacred.**

They are not just vendors—we consider them our production partners, and that relationship is built on integrity.

The oil manufactured at their factory has helped us maintain our goodwill across international markets.

When your name is attached to a product, you only trust the best—and for us, that's Vintage Aroma."

Shashank Rajvanshy
Director, APEX International, Exporters

Chapter 7

Everyday Fats

Beyond the Kitchen

Fats are often seen only through the lens of the kitchen — something to cook with, drizzle over salads, or avoid altogether.

But this narrow view has limited our understanding of how profoundly fats impact every corner of our daily life.

From the food we eat, to the thoughts we think, to the way we age and perform, **fats play a role far deeper than the plate**.

Food is More Than What We Eat

In the ancient sciences, we are taught:

"We are composed of the five elements (*Pancha Mahabhuta*), and we interact with the world through five senses — each one a gateway between the inner and outer universe."

Element	Sense	Input
Ether (*Ākāsha*)	Hearing (*Śhabda*)	Sound, Vibration
Air (*Vāyu*)	Touch (*Sparśa*)	Texture, Movement
Fire (*Agni*)	Sight (*Rūpa*)	Light, Vision
Water (*Āpas*)	Taste (*Rasa*)	Liquids, Flavors
Earth (*Prithvī*)	Smell (*Gandha*)	Aroma, Grounding

What we *hear*, *see*, *taste*, *touch*, and *smell* becomes part of our **energetic digestion**, influencing not just the body but also the mind and subtle layers of consciousness.

And in this interplay, fat holds a sacred role.

A role known across traditions, and now validated by science.

Because Fat Is a Carrier Of Nutrition, Emotion, and Awareness

In Ayurveda, the word **sneha** means both **oil** and **love**.

Why? Because fat **binds, nourishes, protects**, and **transmits**.

It carries:

- The **flavor and aroma** of spices — unlocking their healing actives
- **Fat-soluble vitamins** A, D, E, and K — essential for immunity, vision, bone health, and cellular repair
- **Hormonal signals** that govern mood, metabolism, and reproductive balance
- **Neurotransmitters** that stabilize emotion, sharpen memory, and regulate thought
- The subtle **emotional and sensory imprint** of what we consume

In cooking, fats **bind and enhance nutrients**.

In digestion, they **slow absorption**, improving glycemic balance.

In the brain, they **modulate neurochemistry**, supporting clarity, mood, and cognition.

Fats Are Not Just Fuel — They Are Frequency Holders

They carry **the memory of a meal**, the **impression of an environment**, and the **vibration of a thought**.

From the five elements to the five senses, from gut to brain –

- Fat is the bridge.
- Fat is the binder.
- Fat is the messenger.

To choose your fats wisely is to choose how you *think*, *feel*, *digest*, and *live*.

Cooking: The Sacred Act of Alchemy

Every dish is a chance to choose health or harm.

And fat is the hidden variable.

Refined oils oxidize at high heat, releasing toxic compounds. Single cold-pressed oils, especially those suited for high to medium-temperature cooking (like mustard, peanut, sesame), retain their structure, enhancing the therapeutic quality of meals.

Mustard Oil: Anti-fungal, heart-protective, high in Omega-3
Peanut Oil: High heat tolerance, rich in MUFA
White Sesame Oil: Supports bone health, antioxidant-rich

When cooked in these oils:

- Food becomes more digestible
- Spices penetrate deeper
- Oil requirement decreases due to high bioavailability
- Inflammation is reduced

The Result?

Better meals, smaller quantities, higher impact.

Salads: Raw Oils, Real Healing

For raw consumption, oils like flaxseed, chia, hemp, and black cumin shine.

These are **rich in delicate Omegas and antioxidants that must never be heated.**

Instead, use them in:

- Salad dressings
- Dips
- Morning elixirs
- Post-meal tonics

Why?

Because raw oils:

- Soothe the gut lining
- Balance the Omega 3:6 ratio
- Aid hormonal harmony
- Fuel skin and hair from within

This isn't just nutrition.

It's prevention.

It's therapy through taste.

Application: Your Skin is Your Second Mouth

We forget that the skin is the **largest organ**, and it absorbs what we apply.

Your lotion, oil, serum — it enters your bloodstream.

Which is why we return to the wisdom my first German buyer shared: **"Apply only what you can eat."**

Functional fats like **Moringa, Sweet Almond, Black Seed, and Coconut are ideal for topical use because they:**

- Carry nutrients through the dermis
- Heal inflammation and oxidative stress
- Build skin barrier resilience
- Transport active botanicals deep into tissue

Applications:

- Face serums
- Body oils
- Hair restoration treatments
- Therapeutic massage oils

We don't just consume oils.

- We wear them.
- We breathe them.
- We live through them.

Functional Oils: Beyond Food, Into Formulation

There are oils meant not just for daily use, but **for targeted healing and enhancement**.

These include:

- **Coconut Oil:** Brain fuel, metabolic therapy
- **Black Cumin Seed Oil:** Immune modulation, gut and brain support

- **Chia Seed Oil:** Emotional balance, skin healing
- **Hemp Seed Oil:** Omega harmony, inflammation modulation

These are not cooking oils.

These are functional elixirs, used in:

- Therapeutic nutrition
- Hormonal balancing
- Cognitive support
- Skin disorders

You don't need large quantities. You need **potency**.

And with that, you'll find:

Fats are not ingredients. They are interventions.

Chapter 8

The Potency Equation

Choosing Performance Over Economy

In an age of excess, **potency is the new luxury.** And when it comes to fats, **potency is not measured by price, but by purity, process, and presence.**

Most buyers compare oils by cost per liter. But the real question is: **How much impact does each drop deliver?**

The Potency Equation:

Raw Material + Processing Method = Potency

Let's decode this:

1. **Raw Material Integrity**

   The quality of an oil starts at the seed.

   - **Origin matters**: region, climate, soil health
   - **Storage conditions**: moisture, mold, and time all degrade potency
   - **Seed variety**: not all cultivars carry the same actives (e.g., high Thymoquinone content in specific Nigella strains)

   Check to ensure that your brand vets and chooses its seeds correctly.

   At Vintage Aroma, we choose seeds based on functional value, not just commercial availability.

- We work with farmers who understand the sacredness of soil.
- We harvest with timing, not urgency.
- We store like sages—never letting greed rush nature.

2. **The Processing Method**

   An oil can either retain life or lose it, all depending on how it's pressed.

   - **Cold-pressed = better than refined.** But...
   - **Single cold-pressed under controlled heat = best.**
   - **Rotary press = often a traditional label, but with inconsistent temperature control and multiple pressings.**
   - **Refined oils = stripped of nutrients, deodorized, bleached, dead on arrival.**

   Potency is alive.

   Alive oils retain:

   - Volatile compounds
   - Natural color and aroma
   - Active enzymes and antioxidants
   - Therapeutic lipids like Thymoquinone, MCTs, and Omega-3s

   When oils are processed with reverence—not for yield, but for healing—they become functional food.

3. **Less is More — In Volume, In Usage, In Impact**

   This is the **Higher Profit Model**.

   A potent oil is:

   - Used in smaller quantities
   - Delivers faster and deeper results
   - Builds long-term trust with customers
   - Leads to repeat purchases and word-of-mouth

Example:

- A refined oil may require 1 liter per week per family.
- A high-potency, single-pressed oil may require only 600 ml—yet offer superior taste, digestion, and energy.

Cost per liter goes up. But the cost per result goes down.

4. **Behind the Label — Spotting Real Potency**

Watch for:

- Transparency in batch and origin
- Cold-press temperature range
- Absence of additives, preservatives, and colorants
- Third-party test reports (TQ content, peroxide value, etc.)

Check to see if your brand is transparent in sharing its lab reports and seeds, etc.

At Vintage Aroma, we share our lab reports, our story, and even our seeds.

We want our buyers to **understand the logic** of price, not negotiate for a compromise.

5. **Healing vs Hustling**

Choosing a potent oil is choosing:

- Fewer sick days
- Less fatigue
- Better digestion and cognition
- Higher trust, higher retention

This is not marketing.

This is math.

This is **performance over economy.**

Chapter 9

Nature's Secret to Therapy – "Thymoquinone"

The Story of Kuro Begins

Long before wellness was a trend... before the shelves were flooded with supplements and synthetic capsules... nature had already written her answers in seeds.

Among them was one of her most potent creations — the **Black Cumin Seed**. Ancient, revered, almost mystical in its effect, this seed wasn't just nourishment — it was **medicine**.

Guarded by nature, and whispered about in prophetic texts, the black cumin seed carried within it a compound unlike any other — **Thymoquinone** — a molecule with unparalleled antioxidant, anti-inflammatory, immunomodulating, and neuroprotective power.

But in the rush of modernity, we almost forgot.

Until now.

This is where the story of **Kuro** begins.

The Soul of Kuro

Kuro is not just a symbol. It is a spirit. A guardian. A presence that has watched over the fields of Nigella sativa for centuries.

Silent. Patient. Powerful.

In our world, where potency is often masked by profit, **Kuro returns to remind us**: Healing was never meant to be complicated.

It was always meant to be natural. And precise.

Kuro represents the soul of Black Seed Oil.

It is the unseen protector, ensuring that each drop pressed holds the purity of the seed and the promise of nature's intention.

When we press this oil at Vintage Aroma, we are not extracting a product. We are releasing a legacy.

Kuro lives in every bottle. It watches over its journey — from seed to press, from bottle to being.

This chapter marks the turning point in the book.

We are no longer just talking about fats.

We are talking about **Functional Therapy Oils**. We are talking about **a revolution in preventive wellness**.

And leading this revolution, quietly but surely, is Kuro.

Let us now step into the science, the spirit, and the stories **that make Black Cumin Seed Oil not just relevant, but irreplaceable.**

From Prophetic Herb to Clinical Powerhouse

Across time, cultures, and continents, few botanicals have been as universally revered as **Black Cumin Seed** — *Nigella sativa.*

From ancient Egypt, where it was found in the tomb of Pharaoh Tutankhamun, to the prophetic traditions of the Middle East, **where it was declared "a cure for every disease except death,"** this seed has held a sacred status in healing lore.

But reverence alone doesn't sustain truth.

Science must affirm what tradition has carried.

In the last few decades, clinical research has caught up with ancient wisdom. What sages and seers once intuitively knew, labs and journals now confirm. Black Cumin Seed Oil is not only potent — it is **profoundly therapeutic**.

Black Cumin Seed Oil — once an offering for kings and a cure whispered among healers — is now the subject of rigorous scientific validation. What was once faith-based medicine has become a clinical marvel.

Across continents, from Ayurvedic scriptures to Prophetic traditions, the black seed has been honoured with statements like:

"In it is healing for every disease except death."

This reverence, once seen as poetic, is now being decoded in laboratories.

The Thymoquinone Discovery

At the heart of Black Seed's power lies a phytochemical: **Thymoquinone (TQ)** — a compound with:

- **Anti-inflammatory** effects that rival pharmaceuticals
- **Neuroprotective** potential supporting memory, cognition, and focus
- **Antioxidant** activity that protects cells from oxidative stress
- **Immunomodulating** action that balances immune overactivity (in autoimmune conditions) and underactivity (in chronic infections)

Over 800 peer-reviewed scientific studies have explored the therapeutic range of TQ, with applications in:

- Metabolic syndrome
- Asthma and respiratory health
- Skin disorders like eczema and psoriasis
- Gut health and microbiome modulation
- Depression, anxiety, and neurodegenerative conditions

It is not merely a *supplement*. It is a **functional fat with clinical credibility**.

It has a Multi-Systemic Impact – One Oil, Many Outcomes

Unlike single-function supplements, Black Cumin Seed Oil works synergistically across multiple systems in the body:

- **Cognitive Health:** Enhances memory, reduces anxiety, and supports neurotransmitter balance
- **Gut Health:** Regulates microbiome, reduces leaky gut, improves nutrient absorption
- **Skin Health:** Treats eczema, acne, psoriasis; supports collagen synthesis
- **Immune Function:** Increases NK cell activity, modulates autoimmune responses

- **Metabolic Health:** Regulates blood sugar and cholesterol, aids in fat metabolism
- **Hormonal Balance:** Supports thyroid function, reproductive wellness

Today, Black Cumin Seed Oil is no longer confined to herbal cabinets or religious texts.

It has found its way into:

- Nutraceutical capsules
- Functional beverages
- Ayurvedic and Unani preparations
- Cosmeceuticals
- Brain performance blends
- Gut health formulations
- Vegan omega supplements

Leading wellness brands are now positioning it not as a niche product, but as a **core ingredient** in the preventive health movement.

And yet... most are still sourcing it without understanding its essence.

They chase price, not potency.

Volume, not vibrational integrity.

This is why the guardian Kuro returns — not to merely protect the oil, but to protect its purpose.

The Revival is Here

In the age of antibiotic resistance, lifestyle diseases, and burnout epidemics, we are returning to our roots.

Black Cumin Seed Oil is not just part of the trend. It is anchoring the transformation.

As formulators, manufacturers, and conscious brands, this is our moment to:

- Choose therapeutic over trendy
- Choose functional over fashionable
- Choose intention over impulse

Fuelled by the Spirit of Kuro: Preferred by Our Partners

"For over a decade, we've sourced our Black Seed Oil and softgels exclusively from Vintage Aroma. **What sets them apart is not just the product, but the philosophy behind it—each batch reflects a rare alignment of purity, potency, and purpose.**

From cultivation to container, every shipment has been **flawless—delivered on time, tested thoroughly, and spiritually intact.** Our buyers keep coming back, not just for the results, **but for the unmistakable energy this oil carries.** In a world full of compromises, Vintage Aroma remains uncompromising."

Winston Hudson
Founder, Natural Living International LLC, USA

Chapter 10

Understanding Thymoquinone

The Core of Potency

At the heart of Black Cumin Seed Oil lies a singular molecule that distinguishes it from every other natural fat: **Thymoquinone (TQ).**

This naturally occurring compound is not an additive, nor a fortification — it is a **gift coded into the seed by nature herself.** And when the oil is pressed with reverence, without heat or chemicals, TQ remains intact, potent, bioavailable, and ready to serve.

What Is Thymoquinone?

Thymoquinone is a bioactive compound found primarily in *Nigella sativa* oil and is responsible for a wide spectrum of physiological effects. Scientific studies now show that TQ has:

- **Anti-inflammatory properties**: It reduces pro-inflammatory cytokines and acts at the root level, helping manage chronic inflammation.
- **Antioxidant activity**: It neutralizes free radicals and enhances cellular defense mechanisms.
- **Neuroprotective effects**: TQ has shown promise in improving memory, learning, and cognitive resilience.
- **Hepatoprotective effects**: It shields the liver from oxidative damage and supports detoxification.
- **Antimicrobial actions**: It helps fight against bacterial, fungal, and even viral pathogens.
- **Immunomodulatory power**: Rather than merely boosting the immune system, TQ helps it self-regulate intelligently.

Clinical Evidence and Global Research

Once touted in ancient texts as a *cure for everything but death*,

Rigorous research over the past decades has transformed myth into medicine, and emerging data on Thymoquinone (TQ)—the seed's primary active compound—deliver nothing short of a scientific revelation.

Over 8,700 peer-reviewed studies now explore *Nigella sativa* and Thymoquinone, published by universities and research centers worldwide—Harvard to Hyderabad, Tokyo to Tehran.

Here's what the science confirms:

- A 2021 meta-analysis of 16 RCTs showed black seed supplementation significantly lowered fasting blood glucose by approximately 21 mg/dL and improved lipid profiles, validating TQ's impact on metabolic health
- Animal and human studies demonstrate its neuroprotective effects, effectively treating anxiety, depression, and even slowing neurodegeneration.
- In dermatology, Thymoquinone has been shown to repair eczema, reduce acne, and strengthen the skin barrier
- Gastrointestinal research reveals substantial relief in IBS, ulcerative colitis, and leaky gut symptoms.
- Respiratory studies highlight improved lung function, reduced airway inflammation, and significant symptom relief in asthma, bronchitis, allergic rhinitis, and, notably, pulmonary fibrosis, once considered irreversible.

Thymoquinone: The Master Regulator

TQ isn't a one-trick molecule—it's a biological harmonizer. **Instead of forcing change, it restores balance:**

- Suppresses inflammatory mediators like TGF-β1 and NF-κB
- Enhances antioxidant defenses against oxidative stress
- Modulates immunity—activating where needed, calming where excessive
- Supports tissue regeneration and cellular repair

Validated Benefits Across Systems

Metabolic: Lowers glucose & cholesterol, supports prediabetes and diabetes

Neuroprotective: Supports mood, memory, and neurodegeneration prevention

Respiratory: Enhances lung capacity, eases inflammation, reverses fibrosis

Immunomodulatory: Reduces chronic inflammation and boosts cellular defense

Dermal & Gut: Resolves skin and GI disorders with barrier restoration

From Sacred Seed to Scientific Standard

Black cumin was once a whispered remedy among ancient healers.

Today, it stands under the microscope of science—and emerges with staggering affirmation.

Thymoquinone is not folklore. It's a fact.

A compound that embodies:

- Balance, not brute force
- Restoration, not suppression
- Holistic healing, in its purest form

The black seed has journeyed from sacred tradition to *modern marvel*, becoming one of nature's most profound evidence-based healers.

The Clinician's New Favourite

Functional medicine practitioners, integrative doctors, and progressive pharmacists are now turning to Black Cumin Seed Oil as:

- A bridge between natural and pharmaceutical care

- A plant-based adaptogen that delivers measurable outcomes
- A non-invasive tool for chronic inflammation and immune dysregulation

This offering is a biologically intelligent nutrition, propagated by ancient wisdom and validated by modern science. A therapeutic oil that the world is finally ready to understand.

The era of selling oils in bottles has passed.

We are entering the era of offering healing in drops.

The Potency Gap: Why Most Oils Don't Deliver

Most commercial Black Seed Oils in the market fall short. Here's why:

- **Multiple pressings and solvent extractions** degrade the TQ content.
- **Improper seed selection** leads to oils with naturally low TQ levels.
- **Lack of standardization** makes dosage and formulation unpredictable.
- **Synthetic fortification** compromises the oil's natural harmony and can mislead buyers.

Check to ensure whether your oil is synthetically fortified or nature-aligned.

At Vintage Aroma, we test every batch for its natural TQ content. We do not fortify. We do not refine. We press once. And we preserve everything.

This is how our **2.0%+ TQ oils** are born. Not in laboratories, but in alignment with **nature's intelligence.**

Thymoquinone Is the Future

As the world moves away from reactive pharmaceutical dependence toward preventive, functional wellness, Thymoquinone will become **central**.

It is:

- A **natural active** that fits clean-label demand.
- A **bridge between ancient healing and clinical efficacy**.
- A molecule that doesn't treat one issue — **it restores whole systems.**

Welcome to the molecule that changes everything.

Chapter 11

Delivering Oil as It Was Meant to Be

The journey of Black Cumin Seed Oil—from ancient remedy to modern-day functional fat—isn't complete until the buyer, the brand, the formulator, and the distributor each step into their role.

- Not just a buyer.
- Not merely a reseller of oil.
- Not simply a formulator, a wellness brand owner, or a health practitioner.

Each becomes:

- A steward of integrity.
- A protector of potency.
- A partner in healing.
- A messenger.
- A conduit through which nature's healing finds its way to those in need.

In a world saturated with synthetic solutions and marketing gimmicks, choosing the real oil — the potent, pure, unadulterated oil — becomes an act of courage. An act of responsibility.

Because every time a functional fat is chosen with intention, a decision is made that shapes:

- A body's recovery process
- A mind's clarity
- A gut's healing
- A formulator's integrity
- A customer's trust
- A brand's legacy

In an industry filled with diluted offerings, mislabelled ingredients, and profit-driven choices, there lies a rare opportunity to become a voice for truth.

What Does This Role Involve?

- **Educating teams and buyers:** Stakeholders can be equipped with facts about Thymoquinone, about single-pressing, and about what real functional fats can do. A well-informed buyer becomes a lifelong advocate.
- **Choosing purity over price:** A higher-potency oil may cost more upfront, but its effects are more profound, its usage more efficient, and its results more transformational. Buyers return not because they were sold to, but because they were served.
- **Reading behind the label:** The deeper questions matter: Was it cold-pressed under controlled temperature? Is the oil single-pressed or multiple-pressed? Are the seeds used known for high thymoquinone content? The answers determine whether the oil is therapeutic or merely topical.
- **Aligning with brands rooted in intention:** It matters to choose manufacturers and partners who care not just

about certifications, but about energy, ethics, and efficacy. Every drop carries a vibration — let it carry truth.

- **Becoming a guide, not just a seller:** Those seeking oils are seeking results. The journey includes navigating usage, dosage, combining with other actives, and aligning with lifestyle practices such as breathwork, gut health, and sleep.

The Sacred Stewardship

At Vintage Aroma, the role is lived fully — sourcing seeds ethically, pressing under controlled temperatures, lab-testing for Thymoquinone, and bottling intention into every container.

But the circle isn't complete without those who carry it forward.

When formulators, retailers, and wellness brands choose to:

- Educate consumers
- Source consciously
- Communicate potency over price
- Integrate oils as preventive and therapeutic agents
- Shift conversations from cosmetics to cellular healing

They step into the role of a **healer in commerce**.

This is not the business of sales.

This is the business of transformation.

Every formulation developed, every shelf stocked, every sample shared — is either part of the noise, or part of the shift.

And those reading this are not here for noise. They are here to lead the shift.

The world is ready.

The question is:

Will the oil be delivered as it was meant to be?

The choice defines a brand.

A reputation.

A legacy.

Let the path forward be walked not just with product, but with purpose.

The World Doesn't Need More Products. It Needs More Truth.

This is not merely about selling.

This is about restoring memory.

The body already knows what heals it — this is simply a way of giving it access.

That is the quiet responsibility held by every retailer, distributor, product formulator, and wellness advocate working with Black Cumin Seed Oil or any functional fat.

And when carried out with clarity and reverence, it leads to:

- Long-term consumer loyalty
- Higher margins with lower consumption
- Fewer refunds and better product feedback
- Differentiated market positioning
- Referrals rooted in trust, not trends

Becoming a Bridge Between Science and Soul

No one needs to be a scientist, but understanding the effectiveness of the oil is essential.

And communicating it with conviction is non-negotiable.

Conversations can carry truths such as:

- Thymoquinone's neuroprotective and gut-healing effects
- Its synergy with adaptogens
- Its ability to restore equilibrium in inflammatory cycles
- Why cold-press integrity determines outcome

When understanding replaces instruction, people listen.

Let the Oil Travel Through Intention

In many ways, the one who carries the oil forward is no different from the press that extracts it — a vessel.

Let every formulation, conversation, and strategy be shaped by the same values that shape the oil:

Purity. Precision. Purpose.

Kuro lives through this act of stewardship.

Let every drop delivered be an act of reverence.

Chapter 12

Real-World Business Case Studies –

What Happens When You Choose the Real Thing

While data may inform.

It is the real stories that transform.

This chapter brings to light what **science validates** and **users live through** — the tangible, measurable, and deeply felt outcomes of using **authentic functional fats**, especially **Black Cumin Seed Oil**, as intended by nature.

These are not merely testimonials curated for marketing. They are:

- Lived experiences.
- Field realities.
- Clinical observations.
- Business turnarounds.
- Healing journeys.

Case Study 1

From Doubt to Demand: A Nutraceutical Brand's Breakthrough

A mid-sized **nutraceutical company in the USA initially hesitated to include Black Cumin Seed Oil in their formulations, fearing low consumer awareness.**

After our educational session with their R&D team and supplying them our **2.2% Thymoquinone single-pressed variant, they ran a 3-month pilot.**

The Phenomenal Outcome:

- **26% higher customer retention** in their wellness subscription model
- **40% reduction in refund requests** (due to reported health benefits)
- **Introduced three new SKUs** in brain, gut, and skin wellness under one base oil

The Lesson:

High potency delivers both consumer satisfaction and commercial scalability.

Case Study 2

The Formulator Who Chose Purity Over Price

A leading Ayurvedic practitioner and product developer was offered multiple sources of black cumin seed oil from different exporters.

Despite lower prices, she chose Vintage Aroma after understanding our seed sourcing, single-press integrity, and batch-level TQ testing.

Her words:

"I am not making oils. I am making formulations that restore faith in natural healing. For that, the base must be uncompromised."

She now sources exclusively from us.

The Lesson:

When purity is non-negotiable, **trust becomes currency.**

These stories speak for themselves.

They show what happens when:

- You **do not compromise on raw material**
- You **respect nature's design**
- You **choose function over fashion**

Functional fats are not trends.

They are **tools of transformation**.

And the brands, clinics, institutions, and individuals who honour that truth?

They rise. Sustainably. Profitably. Authentically.

Chapter 13

The Future – Conscious Health, Conscious Commerce

We stand at a threshold.

A shift is underway — from blind consumption to conscious choice, from chasing cures to embracing prevention, from commoditized wellness **to sacred commerce.**

Health is no longer a luxury. It is our new currency.

And in this paradigm, functional fats are emerging as non-negotiable assets.

Black Cumin Seed Oil — once an ancient remedy — is becoming a central character in this narrative. But its success doesn't lie in mass adoption alone. It lies in how deeply it transforms commerce itself.

The Shift: From Transaction to Transformation

People are no longer buying products. They are buying alignment.

They want:

- Integrity behind the label
- Purity in the process
- Purpose in the profit

And brands that deliver that will lead. Not with the loudest ads, but with the **clearest truths**.

Conscious consumers are rising. And with them, the demand for suppliers, formulators, and founders who walk the talk.

The New Equation: Wellness = Wealth

When you create products that prevent illness, restore energy, and optimize brain and gut health, you're not just selling supplements — you're **extending lifespans**, reducing healthcare costs, and building a more resilient society.

That is wealth.

And the ones who bring it forth through nature-backed, scientifically validated, ethically sourced products — they become **guardians of the new economy**.

This is **conscious commerce**.

Not a trend. A trajectory.

Functional Fats as Foundational Tools

As research grows and global case studies pile up, functional fats are no longer niche.

They are becoming the foundation for:

- Preventive nutraceuticals
- Neuro-nutrition and biohacking
- Integrative medicine protocols
- Longevity supplements
- Clean beauty and cosmeceuticals
- Spiritual and mental wellness regimens

And right at the heart of this is **Black Seed Oil**.

A singular fat with **multi-dimensional healing capacity**.

Are You Ready for What Comes Next?

It's a challenge.

To ask:

- Are you building a brand for now… or for next?
- Are your products fillers on shelves, or forces of change in lives?
- Do your ingredients just look good, or do they heal deeply?

Because the future belongs to those who serve.

Not the market.

But the mission.

The mission is to restore balance, dignity, and sacredness to human health.

And that begins with **conscious choices**.

The Rise of the Conscious Buyer

A new kind of buyer is emerging.

Not just a consumer of products, but a **seeker of purpose**.

This chapter is a tribute to them.

Gone are the days when labels alone dictated choices.

Today's buyer asks:

- Where did this come from?
- How was it processed?
- Who made it — and with what intention?
- Does this nourish me… or just sell to me?

We are entering an era where **truth is the brand**, and **transparency is the differentiator**.

From Commodity to Community

For decades, oils were treated as bulk commodities — bought for price, not potency. But with rising awareness about functional foods, mental health, hormonal imbalances, and lifestyle diseases, a silent revolution has begun.

Buyers now seek **alignment**, not just affordability.

They want oils that:

- ➢ Come from a traceable source
- ➢ Are extracted through gentle, single-press methods
- ➢ Retain the active compounds (like Thymoquinone) that heal
- ➢ Serve both *function* and *feeling*

These buyers are building a **community of change-makers** — formulators, resellers, D2C brands — who are tired of shortcuts and ready for substance.

The Conscious Buyer is Not a Niche — It's the New Mainstream

Across nutraceuticals, personal care, food and beverage, and even spiritual wellness markets, this buyer is shaping the future.

They:

- ➢ Read beyond labels
- ➢ Look for scientific and traditional backing
- ➢ Compare potency, not just packaging
- ➢ Believe in *slow healing*, not *quick fixes*
- ➢ Choose brands that stand for something, not everything

If your product lacks soul, they will move on.

If your oil lacks efficacy, they will feel it.

What Does This Mean for You?

Whether you are a:

- Raw material supplier
- White-label manufacturer
- Brand founder
- Retail partner
- Health practitioner

...you must evolve.

Because today's buyer is **better informed, more intentional, and deeply value-driven.**

You are no longer selling oils.

You are selling trust, transformation, and alignment.

And those who meet this standard — consistently, compassionately, and consciously — will not just win business.

They will **win loyalty**.

Chapter 14

Creating a New Market for Good Fats

The world is ready. But the map hasn't been drawn yet.

Creating a market for good fats is not about capturing demand.

It's about **creating consciousness.**

This chapter is your invitation to step out of the outdated paradigm — where price, packaging, and trend-chasing dominate — and step into a **new movement** where purity, education, and efficacy are the cornerstones of commerce.

A More Honest Evolution: From Processed to Natural & Alive — And Toward True Organic

For decades, we've leaned on buzzwords.

"Cold-pressed."

"Organic."

"Natural."

These terms once reassured consumers. But today's conscious buyer is looking **beyond the label**. They're not moved by marketing. They're moved by **integrity**.

They want to know:

- **Where did this oil come from?**
- **How was it pressed?**
- **Does it actually do what it claims?**

The Shift That Matters Now

It's no longer about saying it's *organic.*

It's about proving it's **alive**.

Because even certified organic oils — when stripped, deodorized, or stored carelessly — can lose their potency.

That's why the **real shift** isn't from conventional to organic.

It's from **processed to natural and alive**.

And ultimately, toward **true organic**, rooted in intention and harmony.

What Today's Market Demands

This new era of functional healing demands more than clean sourcing. It demands:

- **Traceability** – *Know your seed. Know your soil. Know your farmer.*
- **Transparency** – *Don't disguise your process — declare it.*
- **Therapeutic Proof** – *Don't just say it heals — show it.*

We are no longer selling oils.

We are **offering tools for transformation.**

Because **good fats are not supplements.** They are **functional foods** — foundational to:

- Energy & metabolism
- Cognitive function

- Recovery & inflammation
- Immunity & gut repair

But Here's the Gap

Unless the industry starts speaking **this language** — of bioavailability, synergy, gut-brain support, and cell-level nourishment —

The market stays **unaware**, and buyers remain **underserved**.

And that's exactly where your role begins.

You're not just pressing oils.

You're **educating a market**, guiding people from confusion to clarity.

You're not just delivering bottles.

You're delivering **living intelligence** — packaged in oil form.

This Is the Real Shift

- From processed → to natural and alive → to true organic
- From buzzwords → to biological wisdom
- From commerce → to conscious nourishment

From Educating Clients to Equipping Them

If you want to sell premium fats, **educate your buyer**. If you want to **build lasting trust**, **equip them** with insight, clarity, and confidence.

A new category of oils is emerging: **Functional Fats**.

These aren't just healthy — they're **targeted tools for healing**.

They support:

- **Brain and nerve health**: through Omega-3s, GLA, and MCTs
- **Gut and immunity:** via natural anti-inflammatories like Thymoquinone
- **Hormonal balance**: supported by essential fatty acids (EFAs)
- **Skin restoration**: through bioactive-rich topical oils

As manufacturers and partners, we are not merely producers. We are **custodians of wisdom** — channels between ancient knowledge and modern needs.

Your brand can become the bridge between:

- **Farmers and formulators**
- **Ancient science and clinical validation**
- **Nature's intelligence and the evolving wellness industry**

When we equip our clients with understanding, We don't just gain customers —

We create collaborators in a movement toward conscious nourishment.

Positioning Oils as Potent Inputs — Not Passive Additions

One of the reasons oils are underappreciated is that they are **treated as fillers**, not **functional actives**.

The new market must treat good fats as:

- Inputs that **make other nutrients bioavailable**
- Agents that **direct the delivery of herbs, spices, and actives**

- Ingredients that **amplify absorption and efficacy**

In other words, oils are **carriers of intelligence**.

And that changes the price point.

That changes the perception.

That changes the positioning.

This new market must be fluent in:

- Phytochemical levels
- Single vs multiple pressing
- Lipid profile preservation
- Absorption pathways
- Synergies between fat types and bioactives

If your language changes, your audience expands.

And this is how you carve out a new market:

You don't follow the demand.

You **lead with conviction**.

You don't compete for shelf space.

You **create mind space**.

You don't sell oils.

You **offer wellness.**

Let us now meet the people shaping this market — the new buyer.

Crafting the Future With Fats

The future is not something we wait for.

It is something we **press** with intention, with reverence, and with wisdom.

The fats of tomorrow are not just healthier replacements.

They are **strategic tools** — for energy, for prevention, for transformation.

In this chapter, we weave together everything we've uncovered so far and project it forward. We examine what it means to create not just a product, but a **movement**. And how the ones who stay rooted in purity will lead this shift from **trend** to **truth**.

Fat Is Not a Trend — It's a Return to Truth

Trends chase novelty. Truth anchors in legacy.

Fats have always played a foundational role in healing, protection, and performance, but the world forgot.

Now, science is merely validating what sages, farmers, and ancient healers already knew:

- That the body heals best when nourished at the cellular level.
- That hormonal balance begins in lipid regulation.
- That brain fog, fatigue, and inflammation often trace back to dietary fat quality.
- That memory, immunity, cognition, and skin health thrive on the right fatty acid balance.

So what are we doing?

We're not "innovating."

We're **remembering**.

Good Fats: Cornerstones of Preventive Health

What we're pressing into bottles today are not oils, but **options**.

Options that reduce reliance on pharmaceuticals.

Options that restore gut flora.

Options that enable the brain to regenerate.

Options that empower consumers to **take health back into their own hands.**

This is the crux of **functional fats** — they are not just supplements or ingredients. They are **agents of alignment**.

They work **internally** and **externally**.

They bridge food and medicine.

They don't cure symptoms. They **support systems**.

This is why the demand for high-potency, single-pressed, clean-sourced oils is rising — and will keep rising.

The ones who understand this are not just selling a product.

They are **pioneering a preventive health revolution**.

Who Will Lead the Next Health Renaissance?

Not the loudest marketers.

Not the most funded labs.

But the ones who protect purity.

- Those who do not dilute, deodorize, or deflate the oil's intention.
- Those who educate instead of advertise.
- Those who listen to the wisdom of soil, season, and seed.

The next leaders in health are the ones who see oils not as a **cost**, but as a **conduit** of wellness, wealth, and wisdom.

The age of transactional selling is over.

The future is **relational**.

It will be built by:

- Educators, not just exporters
- Storytellers, not just sellers
- Partners, not just providers

And the oils?

They will carry not just ingredients, but **intentions**.

You, the reader — whether you are a formulator, brand owner, retailer, or conscious buyer — have a role in shaping this future.

You can be the one who bridges:

- Performance and purity
- Profit and purpose
- Healing and heritage

Let this not be the end of your reading journey, but the beginning of your **legacy contribution**.

Because the future is not built in boardrooms.

It is built in **farms**, **presses**, and **conscious hearts**.

Chapter 15

Epilogue

The Eternal Offering

As we close this journey, let it not be a conclusion, but a sacred pause.

A breath of remembrance.

Because what you've read is not just information.

It is an **invocation.**

Each chapter, a thread in a tapestry woven through time — from seed to skin, from soil to soul.

This book is not mine.

It is yours.

It is His.

It is ours — a collective offering from nature, from spirit, from science.

We are not in the business of selling oils.

We are in the sacred act of preserving memory — of what it means to live with integrity, to eat with intention, and to create with consciousness.

Let this final chapter be a moment of stillness, a whisper to your higher knowing.

A Surrender

"इदं न मम" – This is not mine.

"नाहं कर्ता, हरि कर्ता" – I am not the doer; the Divine is.

"نحن لله وإنا إليه راجعون" – To Him we belong, and to Him we return.

Let this work be a flame that outlives the wick.

Let it travel farther than my voice can reach.

Let every bottle pressed in purity be a living mantra — whispered into the bloodstream, into the memory of wholeness.

We are not just pressing oils.

We are pressing possibility.

We are bottling a promise.

That health is no longer a privilege.

That purity is not a luxury.

That commerce can be sacred.

To those who walk this path with us — as formulators, as healers, as believers —

You are not part of a supply chain.

You are part of a legacy.

We are not building a business.

We are building a movement.

And this book?

It is the lamp at the gate.

Let it guide those who seek.

Let it awaken those who forgot.

Let it protect those who press forward.

With courage.

With reverence.

With truth.

Closing Shloka

ॐ पूर्णमदः पूर्णमिदं पूर्णात् पूर्णमुदच्यते।
पूर्णस्य पूर्णमादाय पूर्णमेवावशिष्यते॥
ॐ शान्तिः शान्तिः शान्तिः॥

Om pūrṇam adaḥ pūrṇam idaṁ

pūrṇāt pūrṇam udacyate

pūrṇasya pūrṇam ādāya

pūrṇam evāvaśiyate

Om shāntiḥ shāntiḥ shāntiḥ ||

That is whole. This is whole.

From the Whole, the Whole emerges.

When the Whole is taken from the Whole, the Whole remains.

Om. Peace. Peace. Peace.

Let's Create Something Potent Together

If this book has helped you understand the power of good fats and the precision behind Black Cumin Seed Oil—or other cold-pressed oils—then let's take the next step together.

Whether you're a nutraceutical formulator, a wellness brand, or a buyer looking to make clear, high-impact choices, I'm here to personally support your journey.

- Need help selecting the right variant or potency?
- Looking for clean, tested batches?
- Want to co-develop a product or explore custom oil solutions?

Email me for a one-to-one discovery session on Zoom
preeti.jain@vintagearoma.in

or WhatsApp: +91 8290365515

I look forward to understanding your vision and helping you bring it to life, with integrity, clarity, and the power of the Blessed Seed and other good fats that nature offers.

Let's collaborate and create a community of conscious humans who nurture and revere the divine nature—and if this book has ignited even a spark of insight or intention in you, I invite you to devote a few minutes of your precious time to keep the torch illuminating.

Reach out, share your thoughts, and let's carry this light forward, together......